CLAUDIO REGIS

SOCIAL NETWORKS AND DIGITAL LIFE FOR PUBLIC FIGURES

© 2017 Claudio Regis
Twitter: @dominiodigital
Email: computadora@gmail.com
Contacto: +54 911 4573 4141

All rights reserved

Cover design:
Silvina Demone de Estudio Vibra

Total or partial reproduction of this book is forbidden, as well as its storage, rent, transfer or transformation in any form or by any means, whether it is electronic or mechanic, by way of photocopies, digitalization or other methods, without the prior consent in writing of the publisher. Violations to Laws Nr. 11.723 and 25.446 shall be punished.

CLAUDIO REGIS

In collaboration with: Daniela Gastaminza
English version: Virginia Sivo

SOCIAL NETWORKS AND DIGITAL LIFE FOR PUBLIC FIGURES

(Survival guide for celebrities)

Dedicated…

To my mother, Susana, who bought me a computer last century. This marked my future.

To Pedro Corral, who kindly allowed a group of teenagers to access remotely to his Apple IIe with a 20-Mb HD when commercial Internet did not exist yet.

To all the public figures I work with every day.

To the millions of people I interact with every day, who remind me that behind each profile there is a human being.

To Olivia and Vladimiro who keep me updated with what is going on in the digital world of kids and teenagers.

Index

Introduction 15

This has not begun just now (A little bit of history) 19

Internet, the eternal memory 21

A word of advice for a healthy digital life 25

To have a website. Isn't it old-fashioned? 29

Recommendations to have a website 31

Social networks 35

    Facebook 35

    Twitter 40

    Instagram 44

    Youtube 45

    Snapchat 46

I want to be famous with the help of the Internet! 47

To make a living out of the Internet 47

You were a great press agent! But unfortunately, I do not need you anymore 49

To be or not to be, that is the question 49

I cannot take care of this! 50

I do not know what to write! Is this okay? 51

Copy and paste everywhere? 53

Shall I upload it now or shall I upload it later? 54

Is this message all right? 55

I have an army of followers!..56

Please! Read what I post!...56

Opening an digital kiosk..58

Oops! I screwed it up!..59

They are killing me!..60

What is the use of having followers?...63

I do not know where I am going but I want people to follow me!.........65

How much for a dozen followers?..65

General recommendations about digital life..67

I want to be an "influencer"!..71

Do I have to be everywhere?...72

Let's go viral! Come on!...72

Television plus networks, the perfect mix..73

But that is not me!..74

We will raffle a pair of socks!...75

Breaking the money box..76

Bye, see you!...77

A round of applause, please!..77

I'm a little scared. There are lots of crazy people out there...............79

I got a "Like"! I can't believe it!..79

Shall I say it or shall I say not say it?..79

Help! The hens ran loose!...80

How about using Photoshop?...81

Come on, it's just a minute..82

She is a great fan of yours! 82

I want my privacy back and I want it now! 82

Shall we tie it up with wire? 83

I want to sleep tomorrow! 84

I am devastated! My cell phone was robbed! 84

Is it useful to have an App? 85

Internet for musicians 86

    Spotify: *89*

Internet for actors and actresses 91

Internet for politicians 93

Internet for journalists, reporters and broadcasters 96

Internet for sportsmen 98

Internet for theater productions 99

Internet for concerts 101

Internet for radio and TV programs 102

General message for all celebrities 103

Useful terminology 105

Twitter de algunos famosos de Argentina 113

Introduction

The purpose of this book is to help public figures: artists, sportsmen, politicians and reporters, among others, to have a digital life as healthy as possible.

These tools can help public figures a great deal but they are also a two-edged sword. If they are not correctly used, they can backfire.

To know how to make the least number of mistakes or how to face a crisis is essential to survive in the digital world, which is sometimes unforgiving.

To ignore what happens on the Internet or not to be alert can be very dangerous for the public life of a celebrity. It may not only damage their reputation but it can also make a negative impact on their career.

All the information on this book is subject to change since social networks are dynamic. Nothing is forever.

The autor

SOCIAL NETWORKS AND DIGITAL LIFE FOR PUBLIC FIGURES

CLAUDIO REGIS

"Millions of people who have nothing to say can now do it on social networks."

(And many of them will talk about you)

SOCIAL NETWORKS AND DIGITAL LIFE FOR PUBLIC FIGURES

This has not begun just now (A little bit of history)

To communicate through a computer, to search for information or to interact with others digitally started in mid-80s. About 10 years before the Internet entered our homes.

Those days are reflected in the 1993 movie "War Games", in which a teenager tries to access the main computer of a videogame company from his computer (an IMSAI 8080 connected to the telephone line through a modem). However, he accidentally accesses a computer where the US defense system is hosted, and puts world peace at risk.

To see the War Games trailer, go to:
http://claudioregis.com/trailer/

In those days, connectivity speed was very slow. The mouse, digital photography and graphic interface were non-existent. Monitors were monochromatic (either amber or green) and text appeared at a speed of 30 characters per second. A primitive world, technologically speaking, which created a new way to interact with the other inhabitants on the planet.

In many countries around the world, there was something called *"Bulletin Board System"* (BBS), a rudimentary kind of *Facebook*. Users could access it by telephone and leave messages on a public board, find all kind of information and download software, among other services. Many of these systems were installed in private homes on Commodore or IBM computers. In most of the cases, there was only one telephone line.

Today it is hard to imagine a "social network" with access limited to one person, leaving a message and waiting hours or days to get an answer. Many times the access hours were limited to the night and you had to try to get a connection for hours because the line was busy.

When Internet arrived at people's homes, these primitive systems quickly disappeared. They were replaced by the new technology. While they were the beginning of the social networks, its access was limited to a group of pioneers, mainly amateur radio operators. In those days, the people who put their computers on BBS mode were called "*SySop*", short for system operator.

A role similar to "*Community Managers*" today, a person or a group of people in charge of managing a social network.

Internet, the eternal memory

Internet has changed the world completely. It has actually changed everything.

It sped up communication times and multiplied knowledge like no other time in history.

To think about scientists connected in real time, located in different parts of the world, was something impossible before the arrival of the Internet.

One of its main changes was the democratization of information production and distribution.

Before Internet mass access, information distribution was limited to traditional communication media.

Today, people can express themselves with the same or even greater speed than the *New York Times*. Anyone witnessing an event becomes a temporary journalist and that information becomes part of the news story that is posted on websites or is seen on the networks, and it also reaches traditional communication media.

The dark side of this is that we often see fake news or with serious mistakes. Circulation speed causes serious distortions.

Sometimes the focus of the information is to make the headlines, to make an impression, and this often exaggerates, distorts or even contradicts the real content of the article or interview.

To be a credible source is enough to make people share content coming from different places without proper verification.

It is difficult to eliminate material from the Internet. If a news story appears on several websites, it is hard to be erased.

There is nothing worse than looking up your name in Google and find out that the first story that appears is negative or shameful. While it is not easy to disappear from the browsers, it is quite simple to remove those stories or pictures from the top places. It is made by including new stories than would displace the previous ones. This will only be achieved if this new piece of information is really relevant.

It is difficult because of the way in which browsers work. Something published by a newspaper read through the country is more relevant than a story posted on one or several small websites.

Browsers assess *(Page Rank in Google)* which sites are more or less relevant based on certain parameters such as: seniority, number of visitors, links to that website and link relevance, among other indicators.

To start legal actions to force browsers not to show that content can take a long time and the consequences are not always favourable. Anyway, even if you succeed in getting browsers not to show that content, that does not mean the information will be eliminated by website owners.

For example, let's suppose they show a private video of a celebrity having sex. They may get Google not to show it anymore but it will be difficult to remove it from the thousands of websites where it will probably continue being posted.

To kill the messenger, I mean browsers, does not kill the content. Though it makes it more difficult to find.

A browser might remove your name from its database but that will not be what you want either.

SOCIAL NETWORKS AND DIGITAL LIFE FOR PUBLIC FIGURES

A word of advice for a healthy digital life

- Do not take pictures or make videos that may turn out to be embarrassing when shown in public. Sooner or later, they will go online.
  See an example of this on:
  http://www.claudioregis.com/libroejemplo1

- Do not take a computer or a cell phone to the technical service store if there is important personal information on it, even though it has been erased. Many times, the technician can recover the deleted files and copy all the information. Do not give away old cell phones before returning them to "Factory Reset" mode and removing all additional memories, if any.

- Do not install applications or software from an unknown origin. Someone could steal information or it could lead to spying.

- Cover or turn off the computer camera when not in use. Some bugs allow hackers to turn on the webcam and watch or tape what they see.
  See an example of this on:
  http://www.claudioregis.com/libroejemplo2

- Do not use the same passwords on important websites.

- It is difficult to remember hundreds of passwords. Therefore, the best thing is to have a single one for unimportant sites and different ones and difficult to guess for important sites like banks, email accounts or social network accounts. To use a single password everywhere will allow those who find it to have access to your computer, banks, networks and other devices. It is advisable to use a two-step security system, whenever possible (together with the cell phone).

- Never click on a link, especially those coming from bank emails. Many hackers create identical websites *(Phishing)* to get you confused and steal your passwords.

- Do not access unknown wireless networks. If you accessed an open wireless network, you should change all the passwords you used to visit those websites.

- While it is impossible in many cases, you should not reveal your location unnecessarily. Many celebrities had their homes broken into when they informed they would be somewhere else. Do not mention where you are going on social networks or other mass media unless it is absolutely necessary.
  See an example of this on:
  http://www.claudioregis.com/libroejemplo3

- There are smart objects now! You should be careful with those devices with Internet access, such as laundry machines. These may let people know when you are on vacation, for example, because the laundry machine is off. Some home appliances send activity reports to the manufacturer.

- Disable the location button or regularly erase the data recorded. All the sites visited can be stored in the device and it is possible to recover the itineraries day by day. Imagine what would happen if your account is hacked and that person can track your steps. If necessary, there are applications that can provide a fake location.

- If you access a social network or an email account from somebody else's computer or a hotel, you should always log out and change your password from time to time.

- Do not share tablets or other devices from where social networks or email accounts are managed, especially not with children or teenagers.

- Check the privacy configurations of all your social networks, especially those on your cell phone.

- Be careful when you unblock your phone by joining dots. The drawing can be easily remembered by someone who watched you do it. There can also be marks on the glass when you write your password.

To have a website. Isn't it old-fashioned?

Social networks being so massive, we wonder if it makes any sense to have a website.

There are many reasons why a public figure should have a website.

Firstly, an official website validates social networks, i.e. links to official networks. Celebrities are frequently victims of identity theft.

The official website is taken as a reference by the media. It must be updated and if possible, it must include the information posted on social networks by means of links to that content.

However, I have got bad news for you:

YOUR SOCIAL NETWORKS DO NOT BELONG TO YOU

Remember that! None of them belong to you. Since you put a lot of creativity and invest a lot of money on them, you believe you "own" millions of followers but that is not true.

Networks are companies offering their infrastructure, which can change the rules anytime or even disappear.

Just as people migrate from one network to another for different reasons. Today they exist, tomorrow they are gone.

Your followers do not belong to you and they will be used by companies to target their advertising. By following you and other websites, users provide information about their preferences and tastes, which will then be used to show them ads.

You must understand that the purpose of social networks is not to be at your service, but to do business with their content.

For example, if you are a jazz singer, the social network system will know your followers like jazz and their place of residence.

That profile, together with information users ignore they provide, will allow other jazz musicians to advertise a concert, since your followers may probably be interested in their music too. Or a bar playing jazz may be interested in offering its services too.

Nothing is forever. Do you remember Orkut, Google's first social network? MySpace?

We must not forget about Sonico.com, which was suddenly acquired by another company and turned it into a dating site called TWOO. The database of the people who had a profile in that social network became part of the new site. You see?

This is why it is important to "suspend" the profiles on the networks that are no longer operating.

You should not eliminate them but suspend them. I mean, you still have them but they no longer appear on the networks.

The best thing you can do is lead people out of social networks to go to your website. Not the other way round.

Try making your own database, get people to register on your website so you can contact them without having to pay social networks. The idea behind social media is that you have lots of followers so you will have to pay every time you wish to contact them.

Remember social networks do not send all posts to all your followers.

Recommendations to have a website

- It should have an easy navigation structure.

- It should contain updated, clear and brief information.

- It should be suitable for mobile devices.

- The links to social networks and how to contact you should always be visible.

- They should include a registration form so that you can create your own database.

- The system should allow you to update the information without having to call a designer every time you need to modify a text or an image.

- The domain (www.famous.com) should never be registered under the name of the designer or the company providing hosting services. The website must be registered under your name or the name of an organization belonging to you.

.COM or .ORG are American domains, even though some people believe they are "generic" domains.

For the rest of the countries, there is an identification code after .COM or .ORG (.AR for Argentina, .BR for Brazil, etc.).

A politician should have a domain ending in .ORG or .ORG.AR. However, they should also have a registration for .COM and .COM.AR so no one else can take it.

.COM or .ORG domains can be obtained at http://www.incrediname.com while .COM.AR or .ORG.AR can be obtained at http://www.nic.ar. In all cases, a yearly fee applies. Remember to renew them and have the contact information updated so as not to lose them.

An international Argentine artist could have a .COM and a .COM.AR, both leading to the same website.

Funny thing: Domains ending in .TV do not mean "television", though they are commonly used that way. They belong to Tuvalu Islands on the Pacific Ocean, a small country with a population of 11,000 inhabitants. Tuvalu government receives almost 4 million dollars per year from those domains ending in .TV.

SOCIAL NETWORKS AND DIGITAL LIFE FOR PUBLIC FIGURES

Social networks

To put it in a nutshell, social networks are systems to interact with known and unknown people.

These are public websites which provide information in different formats: text, photos and videos.

To create a network profile and forget about it or not pay enough attention may be counterproductive. If you decide to have it, take proper care of it.

The usual and almost mandatory mix for a celebrity is: ***Facebook***, ***Twitter***, ***Instagram*** and ***Youtube***.

Facebook

It is a complex system. Maybe the most elaborate social network from the point of view of programming.

The format used by public figures to be in touch with their followers is the *Page*.

If besides having a Public Page, you have a *"Personal Facebook Account"*, your fans may try to get you to befriend them. It is not the same to be just a friend than being accepted into that intimate space, which should only be for the people you know well.

An option to this can be a *"Public Page"* and a *"Private Facebook Account"* with a name only your close circle should know.

This way, you will be able to have a *Facebook* account just like any other human being for your relatives and friends and a professional space for your followers.

As time went by, younger people moved away from *Facebook* and chose other networks where their relatives are not "present" making them feel less controlled and watched over.

While the system allows you to reveal certain information only to a specific group of people, it may turn out to be simpler to migrate to another network such as *Instagram* (also property of *Facebook*) to stay away from family comments. It could be awkward for teenagers to see their grannies making comments on their graduation trip photos.

It could be wise to post one message per day on *Facebook*. But the rule of thumb is: "Post as many messages as you need. It can be one per day, two or none."

Few people will be desperate waiting for you to write something and remember this:

"If no one makes a comment or shares your message, very few will see it. Because Facebook selects the posts to be shown to users and will think that yours is not interesting".

Live videos are appealing and the system itself considers them relevant. You will notice quite a lot of interaction in this case. If a celebrity is broadcasting live, the "algorithm" will select an audience for it.

However, you should not abuse this resource. If you do it too often, your followers may lose interest in your posts.

While you are doing this, talk to people if you can. While you are going live, people can write comments and send emojis. Interact with them, do not act as you would on television, they are on the other side talking to you. Do not let them talk by themselves. Mention them and answer some questions.

If a post is not widely seen, you can always invest some money. The beauty of *Facebook* is that you can widen your target to include not only your followers but another group of people who, due to certain characteristics, can be interested in you.

Segmentation can be done per age, geographical area and interests. You pay by credit card. The disadvantage of this is that the message will read as "advertisement".

Facebook's configuration allows you to post a message and people can either answer to that or start a conversation.

While conversations started by users will not have the same visibility as a message posted by you, it is best that they can only reply to your messages.

However, users can bring up any issue they want, anywhere they want.

I mean, you can post a message about a concert and someone will reply by asking you if you could send a birthday video for a friend.

It is a good thing to allow people to upload images, but you must verify they are appropriate.

Facebook allows you to enable or disable Messages (private messages). If you are a new artist, enable it. All communication is positive. This is the place through which they could contact you for work.

If you are a well-known artist, those who want to offer you a job will find the way to get to you. Your website should always have a contact option where they could hire you for a concert.

To give followers the possibility to send a message and not answer them can be disappointing. Why having this option if no one bothers to answer?

Another alternative is to configure a robot that will respond automatically. You can do this on *Facebook*, the message could read like this:

"This is an automatic reply. We receive hundreds of messages and try to answer them as soon as possible. If your question is about a work project, please send it to contact@... For concerts, go to the following website..."

To enable Messages can also mean receiving sexual propositions, requests of videos with birthday greetings, requests of exclusive pictures of the next concert, requests for help and lots of other unimaginable things.

If you refuse to answer, your followers will release their anger in a message like this: "I have been following you since I was 4 years old, I have seen all your concerts but you cannot take the time to make a video for me? It will only take you a few minutes!"

Of course, followers do not understand that thousands of people make the same request and it is impossible to fulfill all their wishes.

On the other hand, if followers are only allowed to leave messages on your timeline, the fact that their message will be posted together with several other hundreds may be discourage them to make such a request.

Therefore, think twice before opening the private message door. Things may get complicated.

It is all right to have someone to manage you social networks. However, you should **not** assign them **the Community Manager role**. It is not really necessary to give them so much power. This person can do a good job just as a *moderator* or *editor*. Managers can be dangerous. They can eliminate other managers, appoint new ones or directly erase the account. There are many cases of angry and unethical managers who banned access to the account owner himself.

Twitter

This is one of the first mass social networks we know. It allows you to post messages of up to 140 characters, photos and videos. Some of its aspects look like *Facebook* now.

It is mainly to post information or opinions, not so much to create communities though.

It is possible to send Direct Messages here. Its configuration will determine whether direct messages are only possible among followers or open to everyone. You should not allow anyone to send you direct messages.

User's reactions are stronger and quicker than in other social networks. Typically, celebrities snap at one another and scandals are commonplace.

Messages can not be modified once they have been posted. If you make a mistake, you should erase it and write it again.

Account verification (Official Account Check)

A *Twitter* account can be verified to see if it is of "public interest". That is clearly explained on the Help Page: "These accounts usually belong to people in show business, music, fashion, government, politics, religion, journalism, communication, sports and corporate world among others".

In order to have an account, you must fill out a form and upload your ID and websites backing up your verification request.

To get verified, please go to this link:
https://verification.twitter.com/request

On *Twitter*, when you mention celebrities, you must use their user name. That way they should know about it and *"retweet"*, i.e. forward it to their own followers.

If you write **@Celebrity Glad to see you yesterday**, this message will not appear on your followers' wall. Only the people who access your profile will see it. This is because you placed the name of the user before your message.

If you want your message to appear on your followers' wall, you should write **Glad @Celebrity to see you yesterday**.

You must be very careful when writing the user name. There are many fake profiles. Always check it first! You will find a list of celebrities and their user names at the end of this book.

The Acclaimed Trend Topic (TT)

Trend Topic means *Twitter* notices some words are heavily used in certain moments. It would be something like "hot issues".

If you are a TT (for something positive), this can give you visibility and people may start following you.

Many people go to *Twitter* to see what people are talking about in a specific moment and TT is the indicator.

There are trends in cities, countries and even all over the world. User's settings will determine the kind of trend visible in your profile. These settings can be changed anytime.

It can be useful to write about TT or follow highly-relevant issues to gain visibility and followers.

Twitter invented *Hashtags* so users can easily group messages. They all start with #.

TV shows usually choose subjects to create activity on social networks. The *hashtags* appear on the screen so people can make a comment or leave a message about the show.

Hashtags are used by all social networks, but it is more popular on Twitter.

Messages containing a hashtag are easily tracked, i.e. all the comments related to that topic will be quickly grouped.

Hashtags should be as short and clear as possible to have the chance to become a Trend Topic.

Do not put too many *hashtags* on a message. Your text should look human, not a programming code.

Help! My Twitter account has been hacked!

If you suspect your account was hacked because of abnormal activity, it must have been accessed by an unauthorized person who got your password.

If you still have access to your user's account, change your password immediately and check whether there are installed applications that can have authorized access to the account. As a preventive measure, remove these authorizations.

If you can not do it, you will find useful information on the following link:

https://support.twitter.com/articles/371589

Keep your email and telephone number associated with *Twitter* and other networks updated and protected to be able to recover them. Do not use your *Twitter* password on other accounts.

Instagram

This network belonging to *Facebook* is targeted for mobile devices. Each message should be accompanied by a photo or a video. This is particularly used by young people.

It is closely related to mobility since you can not post messages from a personal computer, it must be done from a cell phone or tablet. However, messages can be seen on a PC and you can even write or erase comments.

Community Managers complain this network is more difficult to manage.

An interesting feature is that it can be linked to *Facebook*. So you can see or reply to public messages from the Direct Message section on *Facebook*.

In the case of "live videos", the system allows you to invite members of the audience and splits the screen to show both.

"Stories" is a nice feature to post photos or videos for 24 hours. Disappearing content is highlighted on top of the application. This was originally created by *Snapchat* and it is also used by *Facebook* and *WhatsApp*.

Youtube

It is "the" video network. There are two reasons why you should upload your videos to this platform. Firstly, to make it visible to the millions of Youtube's users. And secondly, if your channel has a certain number of visitors, this can become an interesting source of income.

It is clearly a social network since people can like or dislike videos by showing "thumbs up" or "thumbs down" and leave comments, which can be answered either by the owner of the video or other users.

To get new *Subscribers* is fundamental. Each of them will be notified when a new video has been uploaded as long as Notifications have been enabled.

Youtube grants the audience the power to position your video and suggest it to other users. I mean, the longer your video is watched, the higher score you get.

You should make *Playlists* to group your videos or include videos from other users. It is an interesting way to show visitors the material you want them to see.

I will upload it to *Youtube* and that is it

It may seem convenient to upload a video on *Youtube* and then put a link to it on social networks. But this can be a disadvantage.

Do you think the other social networks (which have their own video platform) will be happy to send traffic to *Youtube*? Not at all.

Your message will probably be shown very little to your followers. Therefore, you should upload videos to each platform.

Twitter does not allow files larger than 512 MB, its minimum duration being 1 second and its maximum duration being 2 minutes and 20 seconds. If the video exceeds 140 seconds, the system can shorten it for you or you can do it yourself.

On *Facebook* videos can be up to 1.75 GB and last a couple of hours. On *Instagram*, they can last up to one minute.

Snapchat

This network is targeted to younger people and uses the concept of *"disappearing"* messages.

The receiver can only see the content for 10 seconds, then the message disappears.

Its future is uncertain. It seemed promising at the beginning but it has lost many users over time. One of the reasons was the introduction of similar features by other networks.

I want to be famous with the help of the Internet!

There are many cases in which this is true and others in which this boosts a career. Social media are usually a "thermometer" that measures the degree of popularity of a certain person.

The most visible case of "Internet celebrities" are Youtubers. Unknown people who created their own show and managed to have a great number of followers thanks to their talent and hard work.

These "Internet celebrities" are sometimes absorbed by traditional media such as radio or TV.

To see an example of this, go to:
http://www.claudioregis.com/libroejemplo4

To make a living out of the Internet

It is possible to make money on the Internet. Many celebrities are paid to endorse products.

The logics of the real world do not necessarily apply to the digital world. The fact that celebrities recommend a product on their social networks does not usually make a huge impact on sales. But this is a common practice.

While it is difficult to reject the money offered to advertise a product on your social network, try to be selective and consistent with your lifestyle.

If you decide to advertise a product people do not believe you use, you will get negative comments and everyone will make fun of you.

Let's suppose a TV star said: "I go to supermarket X on Thursdays to have a 10% discount". That is not believable.

Social networks may help you sell more tickets for your concert or get more people to see your video or listen to your songs, but that does not mean your success is guaranteed or they will help you succeed.

To sum up: social networks can be a source of income. But typically, what makes you earn more money are additional commercial activities, which result from having lots of followers.

What makes the life of "influencers" sustainable is not the money arising from the information posted on social networks but their participation in events and conferences, products and items used in their projects and book publications among others.

You were a great press agent! But unfortunately, I do not need you anymore.

It is a misconception to believe that social networks can replace print media and advertising.

While it is true celebrities can communicate easily through the networks, they do not replace press agents, whose job is to set up interviews and introduce them to broadcasting media.

Neither do they replace traditional advertising. It's just another channel.

Be careful with the messages you post, because they may not just stay on the web and end up on newspapers, magazines, radios or TV programs.

It is important to put together a communication strategy that includes social networks and to determine which of them will have a priority, who will manage each of them and who will check messages. Clearly-defined roles in terms of communication are fundamental to avoid internal conflicts, counterproductive actions and contradictory opinions.

To be or not to be, that is the question

No doubt it is important to be part of social networks. In the case of public figures, it is a way to be in touch with fans, to gain visibility or provide information about their career.

As we have just said, they can also get some money if they are hired to promote certain products or services. It can also be a useful way to thank for gifts or borrowed items..

I cannot take care of this!

It is really important to have a "counselor" or what is called a Community Manager to help you deal with social networks. This person should have good knowledge and experience in communication tools, digital communities and technology.

Considering the perspectives of social networks in the future, it is important that this person should also have some knowledge on photography and editing, not necessarily a graphic designer though. Sometimes it is better to be spontaneous than perfect.

Community Managers should never pretend to be the celebrity in question.

If your CM makes a mistake, you will have to bear the consequences and you could quickly make the headlines.

CMs should sign with their own name or pen name and state this in every answer.

New messages do not need to be signed and if they are in third person, it is perfectly clear it was not posted by the artist, e.g. *"Last performances of..."*

When they answer questions, they should make it clear it is not the artist who is replying, e.g. *"Ticket office opens at 10 a.m. Regards. Sergio (Digital staff of NN)"*

People appreciate sincerity. They do not expect artists to make comments on minor issues. Besides, they feel they have talked to a person and this will create a feeling of closeness, which is what you ultimately expect.

Community Managers should be well-mannered and cautious. They are in charge of your digital communication strategy, they are your representative. Do not leave your social networks in the hands of a fan, a web designer or anyone with no experience in the subject. A good *Community Manager* always plays the role of an assistant, never becomes a leading figure on the networks of the person they represent.

To see an example of this, go to:
http://www.claudioregis.com/libroejemplo5

I do not know what to write! Is this okay?

You should always post valuable information. If what you wish to write is not really relevant, you'd better not write anything.

Videos are becoming significant and they will be even more so in the future. Spontaneous and backstage photos are also significant.

Sometimes homemade videos make a greater impact than a huge production.

A word of advice: Be careful when uploading photos or videos. Watch the whole image. Pay attention to what appears in the background. You may be accidentally revealing "extra" information. Check the content more than once before pressing OK.

Do not forget that posting information on social networks is making it public. Sometimes two photos and one tweet can lead to an article on a magazine.

As we have already said, videos are highly valued by users.

Videos should cause an almost instant appeal. Internet users are not patient with long contents.

Youtube users normally watch longer videos because this is an exclusive platform for videos. But this is not the case in the rest of the networks, so in many cases users will not even be able to guess what the video is about. They will stop if they are not interested. If you wish to upload videos to social networks, they should not be longer than two minutes.

However, if you manage to hold the viewer's attention, your video can be as long as the platform allows you.

My advice is: The shorter the video, the more chances you will have that people watch it through. Do not make it unnecessarily long.

If people keep watching it, it means it is good. If the viewer leaves quickly, the Algorithm *(the software assessing the content quality)* will indicate it was not interesting.

Over 80% of the people watch videos without audio. Therefore, subtitling is almost mandatory. Of course, it is more work but it will have better chances to be seen and shared.

If you record a video with your cell phone, always do it in a horizontal position. I mean, in landscape view, just as a TV set or monitor.

Copy and paste everywhere?

Important information should be posted everywhere. The message can vary though, depending on the audience of each network.

Instagram's audience is younger than *Facebook's* audience. Your message may need to be adjusted.

Let's suppose an artist wants to upload a picture of himself with a 60-year-old soccer player, widely acclaimed in his days but probably unknown by younger generations. This message is likely to be more valued in *Facebook* than in *Instagram*, because most of its users will be too young to recognize him.

Shall I upload it now or shall I upload it later?

One piece of information lies on top of another one. In social media, messages compete against each other.

Your post will appear together with the picture of someone's aunt or someone's dog as well as texts and images posted by thousands of people.

Messages are usually posted while people are commuting to work, i.e. in the morning, at lunchtime and in the evening, after dinner.

So if everybody does this, messages fiercely compete for attention. Just as if all cars were driven at the same time.

Try uploading messages at different times of the day and compare results.

Your posts will not only compete for attention with those of other celebrities but also with the phrase shared by aunt Martha.

It is important to make timely uploads. If there is a big fire in the city, it would not be wise to post something (unintentionally) related to that or a trivial matter in the middle of a public commotion. You should not be considered as "someone who lives up on a cloud".

To see an example of this, go to:
http://www.claudioregis.com/libroejemplo6

Many platforms allow you to plan ahead and choose the date and time of your post. But you should remember the schedule because if there is a major incident in the city/country, your post may seem to be out of line or may be tarnished by the impact caused by that other news event.

Is this message all right?

Most people do not read posts carefully or sometimes they do not even understand what they read.

My advice is to post messages that are short, clear and encourage conversation.

When people make comments on posts, network algorithms consider them important and show them more. A message with few comments is quickly discarded by the network itself.

An image always gives visibility to the message. Therefore, it is important to use them to support the text.

Emojis are nice but they make the message look informal. Do not abuse this resource.

Be careful with the spelling. Fans do not forgive spelling mistakes!

I have an army of followers!

To assume your followers are like soldiers that will follow you everywhere is a misconception. People follow a public figure for different reasons, not necessarily because they are fans or relate to you.

Public figures are followed because of congeniality, admiration, respect, curiosity, professional issues or exactly the opposite, because they reject your views, they want to refute your ideas or they are just trying to hurt you.

There is a case of a young and inexperienced actress who summoned thousands of her "fans" to meet at a public place in Buenos Aires City and nobody attended. Limit your expectations and do not make speculations like this: *"It will be enough if 1% of my fans buy this product"*. Most probably, you will be disappointed.

Please! Read what I post!

Your posts will be seen by some of your followers on their timelines and by those who visit your profile (if any).

To appear on your followers' *Timeline* or *Wall* is a miracle. Some networks are inconsistent. Because though they have millions of users, messages get four or five comments. So where are the millions?

Social media business is about making your posts **NOT VISIBLE**. What?

Networks make money if your posts are not seen. If you want your message to be shown to more followers, the content must be sponsored and that has a cost.

If you want your message to be shown without sponsoring it (though it may not reach all your followers), you must get people to share it and/or make comments on it.

Remember! Networks have an *algorithm* that assesses to whom and to how many people to show your message.

You must get people to make comments on your message so the algorithm will say: **"Well, if people make comments about it, it must be important"**. And if on top that, the message is shared, all the better.

Messages which do not get a reaction will be virtually ignored by the system.

The challenge is to develop interesting content which paves the way for conversation. Therefore, it is a good idea to include a question which encourages participation.

Remember to include photos or videos to make the message more visible. Try not to include too much text on the caption.

Algorithms do not approve of links, since they will make users leave the network and go somewhere else.

Remember that not all networks have the same audience. Try to adjust the message according to each of them.

A word of advice: The more interesting or smarter the message, the more welcomed it will be and the less investment on advertising you will have to make. Networks are meant for conversation so get people to talk.

Opening an digital kiosk

It sounds great! You have got five million followers! But will you be able to get one dollar per month from each of them?

Out of all your followers, only a small amount will have the level of "devotion" required to pay for extra material. People do not want to pay for things they normally get for free.

Young people can be very enthusiastic fans, but they do not usually have much money. Besides, they can always share material. I mean, copy from one another.

To produce quality material is expensive and to make profits is usually difficult. It is easier to get money with a video on *Youtube* than getting someone to use their credit card to pay for exclusive material every month. Besides, followers may not like this move. On digital media, you should earn money without people noticing it.

Oops! I screwed it up!

If you make a spelling mistake, most networks (except for *Twitter*) allow you to make corrections by using *"Edit"*. While you can correct it, previous versions can remain and sooner or later there will be a user who will make a screenshot and post it.

When in doubt about an awful or inappropriate image or a wrong message, the best thing is to erase it.

It is different when you post a message that may harm someone.

If the one who posts the message has a lot of followers, it will spread more quickly. And even after being erased, there will be someone who must have made a screenshot.

My advice is simple in this case, if you feel you screwed it up, apologize for it. Something we were taught as kids. We all make mistakes.

When you post something new, you should check out people's reactions for a while. If you made a mistake or people misinterpreted you, it will be easier to stop or change it. It will depend on the number of followers and how quickly it was shared by them.

They are killing me!

Unfortunately for public figures, all their activities are "debatable". Not only their professional activities posted on social media but their personal life also becomes a public issue.

In the past, it was only the critics who gave their opinion. Nowadays, it is everybody. And those opinions are sometimes the foundation of new stories spreading around.

Nobody likes to be criticized, no matter how "well-meaning" that criticism can be.

Let's suppose someone makes a negative comment on a TV show. A reporter says he/she disliked your play, your performance or you latest album. It is just an opinion, art is debatable. It is not a question of being true or false because art is totally subjective. You think your work is great but someone says "I did not like it".

In this case, it is not gossip or rumors but a review.

There are a few things you can do about it:

1. **Ignore it**
2. **Be mad at the person who wrote/said it and let him/her know about it privately**
3. **Be mad and express yourself on social media**
4. **Be mad and make a hint without being specific**
5. **Take advantage of the opportunity**

To ignore it can be a good option, unless you think you can benefit from making the whole thing bigger. Sometimes the best thing is to let it go, to keep it from growing. Analyze where it comes from and decide what to do:

YOU SHOULD NOT ANSWER BACK WHEN YOU ARE PISSED OFF!

It is not the same answering back to a first-rate reporter on a major TV channel than to an unknown reporter in a provincial radio station.

To resent their comments and let them know does not seem to be the best option either. As we said before, art is debatable.

To be mad and post it on social media in order to get your fans' support and somewhat encourage them to attack the reporter will probably be a lost war.

In some cases, it can be fun or even beneficial. What would happen if you were included in "the worst dressed ranking"?

You can have fun with it, not make it look like something tragic, play with your fans. **"What do you think? Did I look so bad?"**

If you are not a well-known or famous artist, take advantage of it! You gained visibility, they may have even placed you next to a super-star in the ranking.

To get furious and not to be specific about who made the comment can lead to speculations and cause even more problems since it is not clear who you are talking about.

The best thing is to take advantage of the opportunity. They talked about you, they made you visible, you will be in the spotlight. Of course, those were not positive comments, but they have opened a door for you.

Your popularity level will determine your access to mass media. Even though it may not be much, it is a big opportunity.

In the following video, you will see a case in which a negative review became a big opportunity. It had surprising results and created positive content for social media.

To see an example of this, go to:
http://www.claudioregis.com/libroejemplo7

What happens if the review comes from the reporter's social network?

Let's suppose there is a message on Twitter like this: "I went to the theater to see NN's play. It sucks, I strongly advise you not to see it".

If the user is mentioned, it is clear they want you to know.

This could mean they are expecting an answer. Depending on the message, (which can always be misinterpreted because a written message has not tone), you could answer in the following way:

You may acknowledge receipt by sending a "Heart" or a "Like". It is the way to say *"I read what you wrote and I have nothing to add"*. This could also be a way to say you did not like it.

The "revenge" option could be to retweet the comment with an added comment, hoping your fans would come out to the rescue.

The peaceful option would be an answer like "Thanks @PP for coming to see us. It was very hard for us to make it come true. I am glad you were part of the audience."

The idea behind it is "to get him/her off balance". The "attacker" threw a dart and got a caress in return. Reading between lines, it can be interpreted as *How dare you say that after all the effort we put into it?*

The review was already made. The next one will probably be smoother.

Do not hit back when you are attacked. Aggressiveness only leads to more violence. Lie low unless you think this could be used as a strategy to give you visibility.

What is the use of having followers?

Followers are used to measure your popularity. Advertising companies will check this out before offering you a job.

Interactions are the most important thing, i.e. people should respond to messages and participate in an active way.

¡ Your community should be alive!

There are thousands of pages with millions of followers. If each message gets only three answers, that is not good.

If you are not very famous, this will be an introductory letter to those who do not know you.

Your number of followers can influence a Marketing manager (who does not know you or does not remember you) to hire you.

There is not a direct relationship between the amount of followers and positive answers to an advertising campaign. Every case is different. In social media, there is not just one formula to succeed.

In that sense and for your ego, that will be fundamental. But mind you, to have followers is relatively useful, the most important thing is to get the message through.

For you to have an idea, about 1% of your *Twitter* followers will see a post, unless it is extraordinary and very impactful.

Talking about figures: If you have 5 million followers, your message will be seen by 50.000 people.

Some of them will not pay attention to it and some will not understand it.

Do not be surprised. People usually do not read carefully. And some of those who will read your message will not understand it, they will read it quickly or they will be not paying close attention since they will be looking at other messages at the same time.

I do not know where I am going but I want people to follow me!

Remember to mention your social networks whenever you have the chance. Talk about them in every interview and also let people know about your website.

Ask famous colleagues to mention your networks in their messages.

If you are a singer, talk about them during your concert, include them in the printed concert program or use the big screen to promote them. The minutes before the concert, encourage the audience to upload pictures and messages.

If you take a picture with the audience behind (a good resource), do not forget to say *"See the picture on my networks"*.

How much for a dozen followers?

Many people wonder if they should "buy followers". Let's talk about "legal and illegal followers".

Legal followers can be bought by means of tools provided by social networks. For example, in *Facebook* you can invest money to get more *Likes*. These followers are not very loyal. They agreed to follow you and clicked on *Like*. But tomorrow they can easily click on *Dislike*.

To buy "illegal followers", apart from being prohibited by the terms and conditions of the system, is a two-edged sword.

Bear in mind, these followers are not real. These are profiles of inexistent persons and they can be easily detected by the networks' self-cleaning processes.

If you are already famous, you do not need them. If you are planning to be famous, try to build a solid career. You should be able to get real followers without running unnecessary risks, since your account can be deactivated.

"Weird activity" leads to inconsistency and that becomes evident.

For example: You have 1,000,000 followers on *Twitter*, only 2,000 on *Facebook* and 150 average visits on your *YouTube* channel, but suddenly there is a video with 5,000,000 hits.

A quick three-minute assessment will be enough to make inconsistencies evident and detect weird activity.

General recommendations about digital life

- Be authentic. Show a little bit of your life off camera but do not lose all the magic.

- Post messages regularly, make sure they are valuable.

- Alternate types of messages, i.e. photos, videos and live broadcasts.

- Sometimes it is impossible to answer everyone. But if you can not answer anyone or you can not appoint someone to do it, you'd better have just a website.

- Choose a different content for each network according to the audience.

- During a concert, use the big screen so people can tweet and see what other people write before the concert.

- Before uploading pictures to portals, check how they look on computers, tablets and cell phones. Sometimes they look good on one device but badly on others.

- Respect copyright laws. Only share authorized material to avoid claims and a possible account deactivation.

- Do not copy everything others do (not all ideas are good).

- Do not answer a message when you are angry or after you have drunk a lot.

- Avoid arguments.

- Do not post content for no reason, "just to post something". (E.g.: good morning, good evening...)

- Do not buy followers.

- Do not record videos or get pictures taken that can damage your reputation if they go online. If you can not avoid it, try to cover your face, your tattoos. Do not allow them to record your voice.

- Do not share information without previous verification, regardless of the reliability of the person requesting it. Always verify the information before sharing it.

- Do not make automatic posts, unless they are generic.

- Add a password to your cell phone and do not leave your phone unattended. Never take it to the repair shop. Make a copy of its contents and put it on Factory Reset mode, if possible.

- Do not send compromising audio messages through *WhatsApp*. Text messages are easier to deny than voice messages.

- Configure alerts so that you get a notification every time your name is mentioned on a website. This way you can take control of the content online and you will be able to anticipate any trouble. In the case of musicians, for example, it is important to know about unscheduled concerts that are being publicized or scheduled concerts unauthorized to be announced. Automatized alerts keep you from checking the web every day.

SOCIAL NETWORKS AND DIGITAL LIFE FOR PUBLIC FIGURES

I want to be an "influencer"!

"Influencer" is the term used to define a person who has a lot of followers and high credibility so they can influence others. Last century, they were called, "role models". Advertising agencies hire celebrities for their commercials because of their popularity and credibility. The same thing happens online. Influencers can be divided into categories according to the business sector in which they are seen as credible.

The best influencers for youngsters are Youtubers, young people born right out of the Internet. They are well-known for uploading funny videos and have millions of subscribers.

To have thousands or even millions of followers on YouTube, to be a personality excelling on this platform, is not a question of luck.

It is the result of talent and many hours of hard work to write the script, perform and edit videos.

There are "Influencer's rankings" of doubtful scientific seriousness, based on number of followers, message interactions and number of messages posted among other variables.

For example, a popular cook on the web is interesting for brands selling food as well as home appliances.

Do I have to be everywhere?

No. Not all social networks are for all celebrities. Besides, if you open accounts in all of them, you will have to take care of them.

Does it make any sense for a politician to have an account on *Pinterest*? It will not probably be the best network for him.

However, you could "book" a name on as many social networks as possible in case they need to be used in the future. It may be useful to have an account though it should not be necessarily active.

It is not nice to notice your name has already been used when you wish to register an account. It does not really matter whether someone has taken your name or he/she is your namesake, it is a nuisance.

Let's go viral! Come on!

I Last century this was called "word of mouth", i.e. a comment passed from one person to another. On the web, this happens when a comment is massively shared.

Not all content is interesting. People share a post they found interesting for a reason. And this in time, may be interesting for their followers.

The material shared is typically emotional, funny, weird or suggestive. A post the viewer found appealing for a reason.

Before social media, this was shared by email. Who has not received a PPT from an aunt?

While there is some content that can be especially developed to go viral, it is not so easy that it happens artificially.

People do not share everything they read.

If you want your post to be shared, it must make an impact. Another option will be to sponsor the post to force its distribution.

Over 99% of the people are unable to create content beyond posting their pet's picture, that is why they are more likely to share posts. We have seen this for years with remarkable phrases (others not so much), among other useless things on the web.

Television plus networks, the perfect mix.

Es It is the perfect marriage. Television is the mother of communication media in spite of the existence of social networks and streaming channels.

Television is still highly relevant and very powerful to set a Trend Topic. It is almost impossible not to achieve it if it is driven by a popular show, especially on public-access television. You could set up national as well as international trends.

Live TV is not important for young people. They do not watch much television, but they do watch the TV shows that go viral on the web.

But that is not me!

Whether you decide to be on social media or not, to leave impersonators use your name is something you should be worried about.

Do not allow other people to use your identity.

There are many celebrities who do not have an account on social networks. However, there are people who pretend to be them on the web.

There is also the case of celebrities who have an official account and fake accounts operated by impostors, sometimes equally active.

http://www.claudioregis.com/libroejemplo8

Try hard to eliminate fake accounts.
They can get you into big trouble.

Let's suppose a celebrity wants to mention your user name in a message and accidentally he/she mentions your fake account. Some followers may think this is the right one and start following the impostor.

All systems have a form to report identity theft.

If you are using *Facebook*, you can ask your followers to report a fake account. If there are many reports, the account will probably be deactivated.

We will raffle a pair of socks!

Contests are a widely used resource to increase web traffic and attract followers, especially when there is a shortage of original or interesting ideas. It is not necessarily bad, but do not expect big things to come out of it. The risk is that the losers may say the result had been fixed. Find a way to make it as transparent as possible and easy for the audience to participate.

If your followers' average age is about 40, do not ask them to find 5 friends and record a dance video. Though it may be fun, most probably they will not find the time to do it.

Bear in mind it will be necessary to draw up the terms and conditions. And, depending on the country and the kind of prize, it may even be necessary to hire a notary public.

Social networks have their own rules and some actions are forbidden, e.g.: *Facebook* does not allow people to participate by sharing messages.

Read the terms and conditions of each network to know what you can and cannot do before organizing a contest.

Breaking the money box

To get money in return for showing your messages is what social media is all about. It could be a good option if you need to have a greater audience, to reach further away.

A small investment may guarantee your message will be seen by people who meet certain conditions such as geographical location, age, gender, interests, etc.

Advertising on social media is different from advertising on Google.

Google ads show up when people make a specific search and it is much more accurate because it responds to some key words typed by the users.

Social media ads are targeted to people who, given certain characteristics, could be interested in your offer, but who are not looking for the product or service you are advertising.

For example, if you want to promote a play, you should send messages to people living in a certain area and people who like the theater. You could do this with Google by sending an ad to people living in a certain location and looking for "plays in Buenos Aires". In this case, you will pay every time someone hits on the ad. If no one clicks on the ad, you will not have to pay anything. In the case of social media, the ad will be shown to a certain number of people for a fixed price.

Bye, see you!

If you find improper conduct, you should block that person.

Facebook allows you to hide the message. The person who wrote it and his/her friends will continue seeing it but the rest will not. This is the beauty of *Facebook*. Those people will be happy thinking they spoke their mind but no one will see it, except for them and their friends.

To block someone does not mean he/she will no longer read your posts, but most importantly that he/she will no longer be able to write comments on your networks.

If you block a reporter because you did not like what he/she wrote about you, is it positive or will you be giving him/her another reason to continue talking about you? It is a clear way to show you disliked it, no doubt. It is a delicate issue and consequently it has to be handled very carefully.

A round of applause, please!

All of a sudden the world changed and artists who were used to being acclaimed by their audience now receive criticism and aggressiveness. This did not happen 10 years ago. You must learn to live with this.

If the angry message came from a stranger, forget it. Do not let them upset you. If you let them see you are annoyed, they win. The person will be glad to know you got the message. Never reply to this type of messages when you are pissed off.

If the evil comment was made by another celebrity, take your time to develop a strategy.

If the comment was "offline" (radio, TV, other media), you are less obliged to respond than if it was made on *Twitter*, for example, and with an "@mention".

It is important not to fall into the trap of responding to third-party comments without checking who said what, where it was said or why. Sometimes people misinterpret a comment made by someone else or its general context, and that phrase is not what it seemed to be.

If you consider it useful in terms of "gaining visibility", assess the situation carefully before starting a possible war.

To see examples of this, go to:

http://www.claudioregis.com/libroejemplo9
http://www.claudioregis.com/libroejemplo10

Do not rush to answer. You can make a mistake.

I'm a little scared. There are lots of crazy people out there...

Everyone is really brave behind a computer screen. Believe it or not, most cyber attackers would ask you for a selfie if they saw you in the street.

If you are really frightened, go to the police.

In many countries, even in Argentina, there are special entities dealing with this type of crimes.

I got a "Like"! I can't believe it!

People could take a Like as a Yes. If you give a Like or a Heart to a message like *"I would like to have a picture taken with you"*, it can be interpreted as *"I agree"*. Do not send misleading messages.

Shall I say it or shall I say not say it?

There are no rules about what to post or not. But you always have to think about the impact it will cause.

Always remember that whether directly or indirectly, you will be delivering a message.

When you follow someone, you are creating a "bond" with that person. And that may mean something.

You are also "speaking" with that person when you share or Like someone's post.

You are sending a message with every post. And sometimes not with what appears in the central part of the image by with what appears in the back. Be very careful with this. Do not give away information that can be used against you. Your followers are not friends or family, they are strangers.

Be careful with jokes, they can be misinterpreted. Written words have no tone. That is a problem with the Internet, emails, WhatsApp and instant messaging. Avoid misinterpretation.

See an example of this on:
http://www.claudioregis.com/libroejemplo11

Help! The hens ran loose!

A crisis is a moment of anguish and fear.

There are two types of crises. The one you caused on social media and the one you ended up involved in, but which did not stem from your networks.

If it was your fault because of something you posted, do apologize. Show your human side, people will understand. If the whole thing resulted from an event, such as a concert cancelled without an explanation, someone from your staff should explain what happened, not the celebrity itself.

Each crisis is different and there may be several ways to tackle it. It is wrong to think that you will solve the problem by blocking those who write offensive messages. That will just make them angrier. You should use a dictionary of "suitable language", i.e. common words people use for this type of situations, as allowed by *Facebook* and *Instagram*. Make sure that message is only seen by those who wrote the infuriating posts and their friends. People take sides easily. One throws the stone and they all follow.

A word of advice: Make certain the aggressive messages remain unread. Facebook allows you to do this with the Foul Language Filter".

How about using Photoshop?

Digital touch-ups are widely used for improving body parts and removing or changing parts of the photo.

Be careful. If it is not done correctly or there are pictures taken by other people at the same moment, you could be exposed to criticism or even mockery. Remember that thousands of people read your posts. If one of them finds something suspicious, this may become something really big.

To see an example of this, go to:
http://www.claudioregis.com/libroejemplo12
http://www.claudioregis.com/libroejemplo13

Come on, it's just a minute. She is a great fan of yours!

The possibility to be closer to their favorite stars makes people request birthday videos for family members or decide to have a picture taken with them at the next concert.

If you can do it, fine. But if you cannot, get someone else to answer the fan something like *"Thanks for contacting us. We get hundreds of similar requests daily. Unfortunately, we can not always fulfill them since there is not a specific person assigned for this. Thanks again. See you at the next concert. Manuel (Staff member)."*

I want my privacy back and I want it now!

Unfortunately, our society lost its privacy a long time ago. But we are beginning to see the consequences in this century.

Someone will see you on a plane and make a comment on social media.

Last century, celebrities could go places without being bothered. Nowadays, everybody carries a camera around and experiences an unrefrainable desire to post something on social networks.

Fans will not stop harassing you until they get a picture taken with you (in the past, it was an autograph) even though they could see you are having a quiet dinner with your family.

If you are caught red-handed in a place where you should not be accompanied by someone who should not be with you, there will be great interest in telling the story to friends or reporters. And you may even be subject to blackmail.

The life of a public figure will constantly be in the limelight. It is a trick of the trade. Fame has a price, and in this century you need to learn how to deal with it. Internet has changed everything.

Shall we tie it up with wire?

Is it a good idea to post material on a network and have the same message being automatically posted on others?

It is easier. But remember each network has its own language and characteristics. *Twitter* has a limitation of 280 characters, the others do not.

When sending messages to several networks at the same time, remember not all users have the same user name in all of them. So automatic messaging can be confusing.

For example, if I @mention a person on *Instagram* and configure the system so the message will be automatically posted on *Twitter*, it can mention another person because their user names do not match.

To link networks is not a good idea. Take the time to think about each network as a different channel.

I want to sleep tomorrow!

To schedule posts means uploading information to the networks to be posted at a certain date and time in the future. This feature, which originally belonged to *Facebook*, can also be used on *Twitter* using a service such as *Hootsuite*.

It seems to be a good idea, because it allows us to plan for a series of posts but it can also be a double-edged sword.

It is advisable for general messages, but it is dangerous for other types of messages. Let's suppose you scheduled a contest and that day there is a national catastrophe. It would be inadequate to post such a thing.

Let's suppose an artist schedules an automatic message anticipating an appearance at a certain radio station or television program. The time of interview can be changed or it can even be cancelled. If the message goes through, the impact will be negative.

I am devastated! My cell phone was robbed!

To lose a computer or a cell phone with all of its sessions opened, where anybody can write on your behalf, can be disastrous. Not to mention the personal photos or videos that can fall into the wrong hands.

Do not forget to put a password on your mobile devices and enable some kind of remote deletion system to remove material in case you lose them.

Make sure to make regular backups of all content.

Is it useful to have an App?

Podríamos Apps are enhanced websites for mobile devices. They create an icon on your phone and are downloaded from an official store. They are quite useful but it is something else to take care of. Each new network, each "toy" you add to your digital life, is something else you should pay attention to. If the App has not been updated, chances are it will be uninstalled when you run out of space in your smartphone. And if it just replicates the content of your social networks, it does not make any sense.

If you are planning to do it anyway, then the best thing is a free App. A musician will probably find an App very useful, i.e. to sell tickets or merchandising products.

It is an extra element to take into account.

If you wish to have your own application or website, you should contact a specialized company such as www.dominiodigital.com.

Internet for musicians

Internet has revolutionized the music world by changing the way in which musical material is distributed.

Physical records are only bought by fans or given as gifts. But the Internet has brought other benefits!

You do not need to produce a whole record anymore. Today, technology allows you to release a single and distribute it yourself.

People no longer talk about mp3 or "piracy". Music as well as audiovisual content are now part of streaming services such as *Deezer* or *Spotify*.

There are many musicians who want to become famous but they do not have enough talent. If they are only encouraged by friends and family members, and only they speak on the networks, all that online activity will create false expectations. Those musicians may think they do not need to go beyond the virtual world, i.e. hire the services of a record company, have a really good product or spend years on a stage.

To think that the Internet will raise them to the level of a widely acclaimed figure is a misconception. Most of the times their careers will be boosted by the generosity of the users.

They may believe that to be present on the Internet and on social media is enough to be successful, ignoring the hard work and preparation required to achieve that.

That is the reason why it is important to remember that the number of followers does not translate into tickets sold or songs downloaded. I wish all online musicians could be successful. But to become a star is neither easy nor magical. A large number of followers does not make up for the hours on the stage or the dedication needed to become a real artist.

On the other hand, it is true that it will be the first thing a producer will consider when planning to hire you. Please remember: never buy followers. Find them genuinely. There is nothing worse than to be hired based on non-existent popularity, because when the time comes, few concert tickets will be sold. It is better to wait for fame to arrive in due time than to hear a producer say your concert was a failure. They all know one another in showbiz.

Upload your songs to all digital stores. You need to show you are active. At the beginning of your career, you will not earn any money but you will gain prestige and visibility.

When giving a concert, upload pictures of your audience. People like to appear on social media, tag themselves and make comments. This will get people talking, conversation is the guiding principle behind social media.

Make sure you upload pictures during the concert and use the corresponding *Hashtag*.

During the show, have people talk about it on the networks. This will make other people aware of you, who may be willing to attend future concerts or even become fans.

To broadcast parts of the show live is a great strategy to increase web traffic.

If you are invited to be part of a festival, pay close attention to the name of the event. If it is called *"National Rodeo and Folk Music Festival"*, do not refer to it as *"Rodeo Festival"*. Organizers and locals will not be pleased to notice you have not paid close attention to the event since you do not even know its name.

Create special content for your followers, make them feel special. For example, upload an unplugged video just for social media.

Make sure the grammar in your posts is correct. However, do not make it too perfect. They should recognize it was written by you. It is common to see messages that do not seem to be written by the protagonist.

Use your concerts to promote your social networks. Mention them at the end of the show. Make good use of printed programs and big screens.

There is software monitoring radios and TV channels to let you know when one of your songs is being played. This is highly useful, it allows you to take action.

Prepare your own playlists on *Spotify* and *Youtube*. Many people play music while they are working. It could be a perfect opportunity to get them to listen to you!

Remember these systems will also increase your income. Every time someone listens to your songs, you will be entitled to collect some money.

The same thing happens when your music is used on a *Youtube* video. It is your song. Therefore, you are entitled to receive some money.

Promote your music by posting the links to your songs hosted on streaming sites. People under 25 do not usually listen to the radio.

Never let a company manage your networks. They are yours, they belong to you. And everything you do in the virtual world must be under your control.

Spotify:

It is a well-known music streaming site. You do not have to pay per music album or song. Instead, there is a monthly fee which grants you access to millions of songs.

It helps musicians gain visibility. Besides, the counter shows the number of times a song was heard. This can either benefit you or go against you.

You will make money as long as people listen to your music. To know for sure whether what you collect is right or wrong is almost impossible because the platform is not yours.

Share the links to your songs on social media. To create a playlist with your songs as well as somebody else's songs can be interesting. Users can follow a playlist apart from following musicians!

Each playlist should not have more than 100 songs.

To verify your Spotify account go to: https://artists.spotify.com/blog/simplifying-artist-verification

Internet for actors and actresses

Followers like to see personal videos of their favorite stars.

Reach a balance between your professional and personal life.

While you can get visibility with suggestive or nude photos, do not go too far.

If you need to boost your self-esteem and need people to praise your body, do it. But if you do it all the time, followers will find it boring.

If you are out of work, you may want to develop material based on previous working experiences. Or get followers to discuss a topic.

It is not advisable to make political comments. Networks are sensitive to these issues and people will immediately associate you with a certain political ideology. No matter how neutral you try to be, you will always get into trouble. As far as politics is concerned, the best thing is to remain silent to avoid getting nasty comments. The networks are not the right place to elaborate on complex issues either. If you wish to discuss politics, you'd better choose other media where you can really explain what you mean.

Do speak about projects, plays to see, movies, interesting places, among other less sensitive issues.

If you are paid to endorse a product on your networks, try to sound natural and use your own words as much as possible. Followers should not realize you are getting money for making a recommendation.

Furthermore, if you are requested to make a comment about the work of a foundation, even though you are not getting paid for it, make sure to adapt the text you are supposed to say to your own words. They would probably ask dozens of artists to do the same and if all of them say exactly the same, it would be perceived as a "copy and paste" thing.

Internet for politicians

This may be the most complex environment for public figures. But on the other hand, it is the one offering the greatest opportunities.

There will be people in favor, people against you and people fighting against one another. Some will accuse you and some will defend you. Your networks may turn into a battlefield.

The people who do not like you will be there. The big opportunity lies in reaching out to them. The way to do it by getting them to participate, neither ignoring nor blocking the ones who attack you.

The person you address will feel exposed and this will make an impact on him/her. *(Oops! He read what I wrote!)*

Imagine a politician responding to an insult this way: "Send me a direct message with your telephone number, please. I would like to talk to you".

If you call your followers up every now and then, this will create a positive effect. That person in turn will tell his/her contacts.

Make sure you have good filters to block foul language on *Facebook* and *Instagram*.

Share everything you do. Show your human side. Remember everything remains on the Internet. People may talk badly of a politician today but tomorrow they can be their allies. Everything stays on the web. You must be cautious. No one has a right to be forgotten.

Do not block people. You work for others, whether they like it or not. In politics, everything you do will draw love or hate comments.

Be consistent. If you are a strong advocate of national industry, neither you nor your children should be seen holding imported telephones or computers. People notice these things and will let you know about it.

See an example of this on:
http://www.claudioregis.com/libroejemplo14

If you have a large number of followers, you should somehow get them to set a trend on social media. If they all tweet #SmithonChannel4 at the same time, people who are not watching Channel 4 will learn about it. But look out! Think about the *Hashtag* carefully! It may backfire.

See an example of this on:
http://www.claudioregis.com/libroejemplo15

If you have a Community Manager, keep a close eye on him/her. See how he/she deals with your personal account, check whether he/she is aligned with your thoughts and goals.

Once an electoral campaign is closed, candidates can not appear on printed ads, radio or TV. However, social media, being in a "gray" area, are often used to go on with the campaign.

Even if there were regulations about it, it would be impossible to control what voters might do.

See an example of this on:
http://www.claudioregis.com/libroejemplo16

Live broadcasting may be risky in some places, where you can be attacked either in a spontaneous or an organized way.

If it is not urgent, record the message and play it later or resort to "fake live" broadcasting.

See an example of this on:
http://www.claudioregis.com/libroejemplo17

Take the debate to the next level! Talk about your proposals not about your political competitors.

"Big minds talk about ideas, medium-sized minds talk about facts, small minds talk about events and poor minds talk about somebody else." (Eleanor Roosevelt)

Internet for journalists, reporters and broadcasters

Experienced journalists know how to manage social media in a professional way. Actually, they excel at doing this. However, beginners should know that while social media and the Internet are channels to express themselves, they have to be careful. If you work at a mass media channel or radio station, your comments may affect the news company you work for and eventually your future there.

See an example of this on:
http://www.claudioregis.com/libroejemplo18

Many people will send you information. Needless to say, it must always be verified before sharing it, even when it is about a social cause or charity campaign. If you are reliable, everything you say on social media will be respected. Do not waste away your credibility by sharing requests or information without previously checking them.

The first minutes of an impactful news story are filled with error, inaccurate information or lies. Do not hurry up. Last century if you made a mistake on a news program, those who noticed the mistake did not have the chance to magnify it. Nowadays, everybody watching or listening will point that out and will share it if they can.

People like to participate. Whatever you do to encourage participation is positive.

One of the tools most commonly used are surveys. Remember that if the survey is about other public figures, the result can be misleading. For example, if you ask people who they would vote on the next election, the result may not be representative. Internet surveys are mainly a form of entertainment. Therefore, results are not reliable nor they can be interpolated.

See an example of this on:
http://www.claudioregis.com/libroejemplo19

Future journalists should have, apart from an account on the abovementioned networks, a professional profile on *LinkedIn* including an updated résumé.

Internet for sportsmen

This may be one of the most difficult scenarios, together with politicians, given the passionate feeling sports arouses.

Post pictures of training sessions or videos of significant moments for you or for others. Remember historical dates. For example: *"Today is the 10th anniversary of the game in which we won the cup. Do you remember? Were you there?"*.

Never engage in an argument with a stranger. It is a rule of thumb but especially in this case. If people make an aggressive comment, hiding behind anonymity, ignore them or do exactly the opposite, treat them kindly. They will probably stop doing it.

If you are a millionaire, do not show off. Consider that the person reading your post may have to work for years on end to buy the watch you are wearing.

Internet for theater productions

It is not wise to create a website for a performance that will not be running for a long time. It does not mean it is not worth it, but it implies hard work and high costs.

For theater productions, go directly to social media, forget about a website. An intermediate option is to create a simple and economical Page with brief information about the show, guiding readers to the ticket office and social networks.

Shows are mainly promoted by word of mouth. Today, that means social media. People upload pictures and make comments that are highly appreciated by their contacts, even more than those made by advertising companies or the press. Friends and family are usually credible. If a friend made a positive comment about a show, probably that opinion will be more valued than that of a critic.

The important thing is to get people talking.

Flash photography can be annoying for actors and the producers may prohibit the audience from taking pictures and sharing them.

It is important to have certain elements on display in the foyer where the audience can get pictures taken.

Hire a photographer for each performance, to help create content for people to share. Sharing information about the show will get people talking and that is exactly what you need.

At the end of the show, you may take a moment to take a picture with the audience at the back. As soon as they leave the theater, people will like to make a comment about their experience. What can be better than finding photos and videos of that magical night on the networks? They will be so excited they will feel like sharing those moments.

Networks are a convenient way to launch special offers such as 2x1 or "meet the stars" when tickets did not sell as well as expected. It is the only way to make those special offers widespread quickly. All queries must be answered. All of them. The networks are used to provide information about the play and can be supplemented with videos of the characters, director, stage designer, producer, among others. A feeling of intimacy between the producers and the audience can even get people to go see the performance again.

Post an event and share it. For example, the birthday of one of the actors.

Internet for concerts

Concerts are usually promoted on the artist's networks, except when they are held abroad. In that case, the production company will publicize the event on their website to make sure people buy tickets. Their efforts will probably be greater that the ones made by the artists themselves.

In the past, you were not allowed to take pictures in concerts. Nowadays, producers do not make this request because it is something almost impossible to control. Everyone in the audience has a cell phone and many of them will probably record a video or take a picture.

It is difficult to understand why someone would prefer to see the show through a camera instead of enjoying the moment. But this is what usually happens in all kinds of shows, even with audiences of different ages.

Some people may even broadcast live the whole show or part of it, to share it with their followers, something nobody could think of a few years ago.

If someone uploads a concert video on the web and you do not want it to become widespread, remember all systems have the possibility to report this so this material can be removed.

It is hard to pinpoint what helps promote a concert and what spoils the surprise.

Internet for radio and TV programs

When there are new TV channels or radio stations, the old ones change a lot. Use Internet services to promote your product. Use the networks to receive feedback from the audience, announce future programs and share news that can be interesting for your viewers or listeners.

If you have a "niche" program such as a weekly fishing show, post relevant information every week. It is a way to keep in touch with your followers.

When the program is about to be aired, make a comment on your networks to attract more followers.

After the program is aired, you could upload the whole thing or the most important interviews to *Youtube* and you could get some money from it.

Streaming channels allow viewers to rewind or go forward. This can be detrimental to sponsors since the audience will be skipping their ads.

Be creative. Online content should not compete with live shows. The whole idea behind this is to allow viewers to catch up on what they missed. If you can not upload the material, somebody else can do it for you. However, you should have control over that person.

General message for all celebrities

You have been blessed with an extraordinary power to help people out. Make good use of it.

Your fans will follow you and you can easily reach them through social media.

Encourage them to help people in need, victims of natural disasters, schools, etc.

Your name can open doors. Besides, as an added benefit, this will provide valuable content to your networks. The cost is almost none and the results can be incredible. Get involved! You are not supposed just to share messages from somebody else. The impact will be quite different if you become the leader of a humanitarian campaign. Record a video. Let people see you. Set yourself as an example for fans as well for colleagues.

http://www.claudioregis.com/casolorena

Useful terminology

Social media and the Internet have their own terminology. There are hundreds of words and expressions. These are some of the ones you need to know:

URL Shortener:
Websites allowing to convert a long Internet address into a shorter one. You can post messages that look tidier and use fewer characters.
Some of these are: Bit.ly, cor.to, tintyurl.com, etc.

Ad Words (Google):
Google's advertising platform.

Algorithm in social media:
Software making decisions based on some of the characteristics of the message posted. For example, it decides how many users should see it or who should see it.

Organic scope:
The number of people who get to see a message spontaneously, i.e. when there is no money involved. It relies on the algorithm decisions.

App:
Short for Application. Program that can be downloaded to mobile devices freely or for a fee. Once it is installed, you will see an icon on your cell phone screen or tablet.

@mention:
Mention a person by using his/her *Twitter* user name.

QR Code:
A graph captured by a mobile device whose information is decoded by a special software. It is mainly used to avoid taking notes or printing stuff.

Community Manager (CM):
Person who manages an online community. Their main duty is to produce online material (i.e. text, photos, graphs and videos), develop strategies, answer followers and advice celebrities on their digital life. This person must be available 24/7.

CPC:
It means "cost per click". The amount of money you will have to pay every time a person clicks on your ad.

CPM:
The amount of money you will have to pay after your ad has appeared a thousand times.

Domain:
The name under which a website and/or an email account is registered.

E-commerce:
Online commerce. Goods sold over the Internet.

Email Marketing:
Information about products or services sent by email.

Engagement:
A sense of "belonging" between followers and a brand or a person.

Fan page:
Name given by *Facebook* to a Page which has followers. Unlike a Personal Profile, you do not befriend people. Fans decide to follow a celebrity.

Followers:
People following a user on social media.

FTP:
Protocol used to send or modify a website.

Geolocation:
To mention a person's geographical location.

Animated GIF:
Moving image format.

Google+:
Google's proprietary social network.

Hacker:
Person who gains access to information or to a device without the authorization of the user.

Hangouts:
Google service for instant messaging and videoconference.

Hashtag:
A tag made up of a word or phrase (without space) preceded by the number sign (#). It helps people group messages included in a specific tag.

Hosting:
Service allowing users to store websites and emails. It usually has a monthly fee.

HTML:
HyperText Markup Language used to create websites.

Influencers:
People with a large number of followers and a high degree of credibility capable of influencing others with their opinions or views.

Keywords:
Words defining the main characteristics of web content.

Millennial (Generation Y):
People born between 1980 and 1995.

LinkedIn:
Network bought by Microsoft which allows people to upload résumés, set up professional relationships and follow companies or organizations to be informed about job openings.

Page Rank:
A 1-10 scale used by Google to rate a website in terms of relevance. The highest the score, the highest place on the search engine.

Phishing:
Method used by criminals to deceive users in order to gain access to their personal data. They usually send an email with a link to a fake site, with a similar design to the original one in order to obtain passwords and credit card numbers. Never send personal information by email nor access websites such as banks or product sale pages from a link you receive by email or through an unreliable website.

Plandid:
Planned photography in spite of looking spontaneous.

Streaming:
The way in which audio or video content (either live or recorded) is played while being downloaded. Netflix and Youtube are examples of video streaming while Deezer and Spotify are examples of audio streaming.

Troll:
This term is used to refer to a provoking user, one that bothers others because he/she gets pleasure in doing so.

Tweet:
Message published on Twitter of up to 280 characters.

Account verification:
Identification provided by social networks, usually to public figures and brands, which indicates that an account really belongs to that person. There is a blue check next to the user name.

Virality:
Mechanism by which a message is shared from one user to another. In the real world, it is called "word of mouth".

Youtuber:
People who create videos for Youtube on different subjects. The ones who become popular can make a living out of this, by getting sponsors and/or getting paid for their material.

Printed in Great Britain
by Amazon